DHARMA IN ECONOMICS KINDLING INTROSPECTION

DHARMA IN ECONOMICS KINDLING INTROSPECTION

GADHADHARAN PUNATHIL

Unity of Humanity Under The agesis of
God on the yardstick of Dharma /
Righteousness or to simply put it Good
pure and simple.

Contents

Foreword   vii

Preface   ix

Acknowledgements   xi

Prologue   xiii

  1. Chapter 1   1

Foreword

Economics is a supposed science for bringing about the professed disposition of fair & reasonable distribution of worlds wealth so as to provide conditions necessary for enabling humanity to cater to its needs of having a comfortable living and a happy disposition making it conducive to the maintenance of an atmosphere augmenting progress of humanity in peace to yonder lofty levels. Unfortunately nowadays one realizes that economic principles are stultified and are really in practice for achieving the opposite effect resulting in concentration of wealth in the hands of a few and resultant slavery-like situations in miseries to the General public. Applying the age old concept of all-pervading Dharma meant for good of humanity in all spears for evaluating Economics One comes to the reality that almost all good basic principles are subverted so as to achieve concentration of wealth and money in the hands of a few making the rest of general humanity a sphere to augment & safeguard these wealthy classes' wealth and power in near slavery & miseries. This brings in the compulsory necessity of a rethinking and introspection of economics as is practiced nowadays in order to make it in accordance with the professed purposes for which it has been brought into existence. The author attempts to evaluate and ignite these introspections so as to bring about economic good for all humans ensuring realization of tall claims of economic equality and freedom as are necessarily enshrined in the Basic rights as is inherent in the Civilised Democratic rights of a free and reasonably fair world.

Preface

Here one finds The author evaluating the economics and economic principles employed mainly intending the achieving of fair and reasonable living conditions for the general public and humanity in general going against the professed purpose and bringing in adverse effects stultifying fairness and reasonableness in wealth distribution resulting in a near-slavery and exploitative situation for the general public, especially the common man. The author's attempt is to ignite an introspection on the present practicalized economics so as to make the purpose and intention of bringing about Economics for humanity's good a reality.

Acknowledgements

" Eshwara Guruvea ". " God The Teacher ".

Prologue

Economics as all are aware is the science dealing with the accumulation sustenance distribution and management of wealth for the good of humanity. Nowadays when even the progress of a human being is measured in terms of the wealth and money earned and accumulated even if there are enormous contributions for the betterment of humanity or human beings. It dawns on everyone and becomes obvious that Economics is assuming primary importance nowadays and touches everyone's life's basically even to the extent of paving the ways of one's life's ways and goals. Anyone with prudence and commonsense can easily understand the Economic concepts on which the money market and wealth are managed so as to make it available to all basically as human beings equally for a comfortable living. With a little introspection and reasoning powers anyone one can read and understand the purpose and aims of economics and Economic principles coming into being and the purpose for which Economics manifest. Anyone can by rubbing these dispositions enumerated by The author on the touchstone of reasonable Good of humanity and effect brought about understand and assess whether these principles intended for securing the best for the general public or humanity at large are actually achieving the intended results for which they are brought into being and employed. The readers are left to draw their own assumptions in accordance with the perceptive powers God bestowed in coming to conclusions about the need to bring in necessary changes for the good of humanity.

CHAPTER ONE

should be A science or a concept bringing into being a proposition for adherence has to be necessarily and compulsorily be for the good of Humanity especially if these principles have to be acceptable and adhered to by Humanity in general. It is a futile moronity to pursue a way or purpose bringing in perils miseries and catastrophes to humanity in general. Unity of humanity cannot be brought about and will not be able to be made a reality on a concept or goal which is not good for humanity or which brings in bad or evil results bad for humanity. These bring one to the awkward situation wherein when there are two results that will manifest in following a way in two different manners that which ensures good outcome is preferred to the one that brings in bad. This situation of two results one good and the other bad by following a way in a slightly different method necessitates the eschewing of the way that brings in bad or evil consequences. The prohibition of pursuing the method of bringing in bad results is achieved by making the way of evil a punishable offense thereby putting a deterrent on anyone who intentionally dares in that way making it not al; all attractive or profitable. These are the basic necessaries required in nay society or the world at large so as to ensure the progress of humanity in prosperity peace and happiness to lofty levels. With these, it becomes obvious that these basic essentials have to be adhered to for achieving the bringing about of economic Justice creating an atmosphere and disposition conducive for human beings to excel in the pursuit of their respective fields thereby contributing to hastening the catapulting of humanity as a whole to the ultimate progress achievable. Economic Justice implies that all human beings are basically equal irrespective of their wide differences as to capacities, capabilities aspirations, and responses, as well as necessities, and are entitled to be assured the basic requirements for a reasonably good life without any difficulties for food, clothing, and shelter. Economics as a science nowadays is supposed to contribute to these goals of humanity essentially by regulating the wealth of the world so as to ensure that all human beings get a fair and reasonable means for their living so as to make them competent to strive further in excelling in their respective spears of activities augmenting the general well being and progress of humanity in peace and prosperity to yonder heights. As a corollary Economics is a science dealing with the ways for the bringing about of economic well-being of humanity as a whole regulating the creation, accumulation, distribution, and sharing of the world's wealth for the common good of humanity.

The predicament ignites and crops up when economic concepts and instruments of money market manipulations intended to achieve results conducive to the good and reasonable equality are distorted and manipulated by vested interests so as to make it an ostensible method for achieving the professed aims but in reality achieving the malady of concentration of wealth in the hands of few. The issue becomes more reprehensible and takes an evil turn when one finds that principles of Economics are distorted and made use of to suit the necessities of a group of people mainly abused intending to safeguard their wealth and interests in the process making it adverse to the vast majority thereby converting the general public a source of earning wealth by exploitation and economic slavery. Abuse of Economics and application of principles of economics for bringing about a consequence that is not intended by the concept of economics converts the vast General public into scapegoats for exploitation securing the safeguarding of the minority's wealth accumulation, safeguarding, sustenance increasing, and prominence thereby pushing the vast general public or humanity into perils, difficulties, poverty and miseries without even able to bolster up the bare necessities for a decent living. These realities become more evident and manifest when one considers the reality of present day times of say about three thousand or so billionaires controlling the majority of the world's wealth and the rest of humanity becoming or being made a group for supporting these evil and deceptively fraudulent tactics of the few minorities. It is in these contexts that one has to view Dharmaism as a socio-political-economic concept intended to revolutionize the good of humans and humanity. The importance of these realities crops up alarmingly when one comes to know that the majority of the world's population of say eight billion controls or has access to only a minor percentage of the total wealth and processes for means to achieve wealth. Even in supposedly developed nations of the world like the United States of America, people are in poverty and misery going about like donkeys in pursuit of mirages of financial prominence and dreams floated by cunning billionaires meant only for the purpose and ways of the rich class ensuring only miseries and poverty to common people. Viewing these in the .of the latest exposition that The United States Of America where Capitalism is being hardently espoused and adhered to is not within the first fifteen nations of the world Where living is pleasant happy and people-friendly. The truth is that the economic management in U S A is not up to the mark as it is furthering the disparity of wealth and income distribution for its citizens to a chasmic level. Almost all Constitutions of the World's Great nations make tall claims and broad propositions Stipulating of Economic equality as the main purpose for which Governments should strive or persevere and achieve. These are with the Good intention of providing all with adequate means or reasonable provisions for having basic necessities as well as comforts in life enabling everyone to have a decent standard of living providing emphasis on senior citizens who have toiled all their life contributing to the progress in peace and prosperity of humanity.

In going by the essential yardstick for science taking Economics as science intended to bring about a basically equal and fairly reasonable distribution of the world's wealth for ensuring a decent and comfortable for all one comes face to face with the present time's economic reality of concepts of economics and ways stultified and distorted even to the extent of negativeing common sense corollary thereby ensuring only the security multiplication and the quadrupling of the wealth of the wealthy and rich few in the world bringing about a paradox not intended by economics as science intended for social reform meant for bringing about healthy and happy living standards or standard of living conditions in a country or world at large. Thus economics is the science that postulated as to how the money market should be molded in a country so as to achieve the possible best living standards ensuring the eradication of exploitation of anyone for subserving the cause or purpose of another. Economics as a science dealing with the management of wealth in societies has to see to it that whatever ways and objects are adopted pursue and employed should necessarily and compulsorily bring in the Good of all in that all and everyone should get " Reasonable returns "for their efforts wherever however or in whatever legally permissible ways and means adhered to. Only this will bring in a real sense of economic equality in practice as well as disposition. Thus labor putting in his efforts of work sincerely day to dusk should get reasonably fair wages incommensurate to his work put in simultaneously securing reasonable returns for his employer for his money expended. These Quid Quo pro reasonable returns should be ensured and secured to each and everyone for their sincere and faithful work. A Billionaire putting in huge capital for innovation and innovative enterprise has to get a reasonable return for his entrepreneurship and enterprise. Only undue exploitation and slavery should be curtailed and averted.As are the realities Economics combined with statistics has br4ought out ways for predicting to a reasonably fair level of certainty The demand necessities of people as well as other economic realities affecting everyday life.These possibilities have brought in hordes of interest in economics by vested interests intending to make a quick buck resulting in the stultification of economic theories and instruments distorting it to the extent of even going against the defined purposes of economics and commonsense and abusing it with impunity so as to achieve their antisocial objects thereby securing the wellbeing and welfare of a small section of society to the detriment of the general public.These abuses can be deciphered every day by just going through the tall claims Of Nations finance departments and instrumentalities of their policies resulting in difficulties for the general public as is evident from the sudden price rise of essential commodities and interest rates including public utilities services in the name of controlling inflation and thereafter coming with the proclamations of rising inflation recession etc.This manifests even though The finance ministries of Great nations are manned by persons who have doctorate degrees in economics who are going by the parrot learned stultified theories intended to benefit only the rich and super-rich even without subjecting these to testing on the touchstone of reason and the ultimate goal of good of people. Persistently going by the untested parrot learned stultified theories of money market controls for containing inflation and curtailing recession without introspection even when manifest doubt and impracticality crops up is unfit for a prudent and reasonable person or persons with commonsense. Capitalism is propagated by the United States of America vigorously and in present times one finds India going forcibly on capitalist lines completely privatizing or attempting to privatize even public utility services or basic essential services which every democratically elected people's government is duty-bound to provide to its people mainly saying that its all loss incurring concerns burdensome placing the common people and governments on a disadvantage causing huge financial losses and inconveniences to people. Everyone has a right to freedom of movement to any part of India unless regulated or prohibited by reasonable necessity in public interests. On assuming that freedom of movement is a cardinal and necessary freedom in a democracy enabling people to meet their loved ones and acquaintances and also to carry on their avocations for earning a living or socializing so as to be necessary for maintaining the well being welfare and happiness of the people generally it becomes as a corollary that One of the Governmental duties is to secure and provide to the people a reasonable and fair means of travel or movement for its people.These assertions are substantiated by the reality that in India wrongful restrain of anyone's movement or travel is an offense under Section 339 of the Indian Penal Code w2hch says that -Whoever voluntarily obstructs any person so as to prevent that person from proceeding in any direction to which that person has right to proceed is said to wrongfully restrain that person Section 440 makes it punishable to wrongfully restrain any person as an offense punishable with up to one month simple imprisonment or with fine up to five hundred rupees or with both. Nowadays even the essential services supporting and making the reality the right of movement namely public transportation services The Governments are privatizing pushing the General public into the hands of private entrepreneurs who are fueled and moved only by profit motives of increasing their profit margins. The right to travel of the people is placed exclusively in thehands of private enterprises who are moved only by profit motives without Governemtal controls brings in the evils of exploitation and ravage of the right of freedom of movement thereby causing untoward difficulties to people of having to pay through the nose for exercising one of their essential and basic rights. An entrepreneur or businessman or any other person engaged in trade and commerce is basically trained and is moved or propelled by the only motive and ultimate aim of profits and only profits whatever. In contra to these is the reality that is to be actually achieved by the purposes and object intended by democracy to be achieved as is propagated and rampantly sought to be enforced with impunity by almost all the nations of the world. Democracy is rule by the people for the Good of the people bringing in the underlying necessity that the choosing of the people's representatives by the universal adult franchise of democratic concepts and aims when practicalized has to be necessarily and compulsorily aimed with an object or goal of achieving Good of people augmenting peaceful progress in prosperity and happiness. The purpose and goal of democracy is thus being the achievement of The Good of the people profit motives or the quest for profits and balance sheet showing huge reserves and profits without matching services to augment peoples rights go contrary stultifying democratic norms and aspirations hampering people's good.

When Governmental organizations and Governments give up Utility services in the name of profits and profitability to private enterprises. Isn't it an abdication of their basic duties enjoined upon them being a democratically elected people's Governments with the only purpose and aim of securing the striving and persevering for the Good of The People safeguarding their freedoms and well being. These assume more importance and prominence when one comes to know or realizes the reality that Politics is Striving persevering or simply working for the good of a Nation (National Politics) When it's working or persevering for the good of a District it's District Politics and so on and so forth as a corollary ultimately it is World Politics that is striving and persevering for the Good and well being of The world. These bring one face to face with the reality and concern that as Politics is Persevering for the Dharma of the world or a Nation as the case may manifesting the cardinal duty in politics essentially being Good of people and not profit motives, Whether an entrepreneur or anyone more concerned with profit motives can really manage a nation or The World as a company working or going about as managed by trained entrepreneurs with the only aim and purpose of profits. Any prudent person with common sense can very well easily on a consideration of these basic differences come to the conclusion that an entrepreneur or a business person is incompetent to manage the economy of a Nation or world except when he alters his ways means purpose and orientation from Profit motivated to " Good of people and Humanity" .If this metamorphosis is not there no one can manage nor be competent to be in the helms of affairs of any concern or specifically a Government concern engaged in and striving to secure the welfare wellbeing and Goof of People of people or the affairs of the country or world.Essentially what one has to look for In Governmental organizations and agencies for ascertaining their competence is whether their ways, means and object are motivated by the business-like Profit oriented, centered Motives or is it Service orientation. This yardstick of Good of people is the determining factor entitling anyone or everyone to be competent for service to people in Government and Governematnal agencies intended and brought into being to strive and persevere for the Good of people. Capitalism is moved and ignited by the sole criteria of makign a profit whatever or in however manner possible. This one finds in capitalist oriented countries like United States Of America etc where one finds rampantly that One is encouraged to charge a fee or price even form talkig with another person thereby bringing in the commercialization of even personal private affairs and human relationship. In societies like these one finds that The progress capacities or capabilities of One and anyone is measured in terms of the money or wealth earned by the person unmindful of the ways and means of how money is earned or accumulated and not by his contributions for the Good and betterment of humanity or society. This unconcern of how and by what means money is earned brings in the evil of encouragement of accumulating wealth and money by evil adharmic ways and means adding to the already chaotic and perils leading to rampant criminalization bringing about consequent implosion going to the extent of as correctly put in by Respected Justice Late Mr V.R Krishnaiyer in a supreme court of India Judgement dealing with granting of maintenance to a divorced lady finding that she has no means to maintain herself and holding that if MAINTRAINCANCE IS NOT ALLOWED SHE WILL " Have to Renounce her Soul and sell her Body " for existence. These espouse the reality that people will go to any extent to earn only to the extent of selling their bodies after renouncing their souls thereby pushing all to extreme degradation and evil. Renouncing The Soul is used in the context of bringing about the possibility of extreme levels of evil that anyone can go to or fall to. The soul is the particle of God within a human being wedded to Good unconcerned by anything else. When Soul gets detached from oneself The human being is no more and only a dead body remains which will after some time get merged into the soil. Without Soul or renouncing one's soul makes oneself evil and diabolically cruelly inhuman. The voice of the soul can be heard by anyone and everyone when one thinks of or endeavors to do bad things one can know the soul saying no it's bad but blinded by desires and the yearning to get that which is not that of oneself one goes ahead and does bad things. This is the voice of the soul. When this voice of restain is not there or renounced one will succumb to unfathomed depths of evil and inhumanness prone to evil activities. These are enumerated to bring in the divinity of being or in a human being stressing the fact of there being a Good orientation pervading naturally and basically in everyone who is human. This natural instinct should be there manifestly more in people making Government and governmental agencies so that evil can be eschewed and peoples good perpetrated rampantly. These come in handy in assessing the qualities and qualifications necessary for people manning public offices so as to make these organizations brought into being for the public good more vibrant and effective for the cause of being brought into existence. These are handy in helping the assessment of capitalism in achieving the realization of the rising of humanity to yonder levels of progress contemplated. Humans are as everyone knows coming together of the natural elements and the particle fo God bringing in a sense of sacredness and divinity to every human being. Holy Bible says that God created human beings in God's own resemblance thereby further buttressing the sense of divinity inherent in any and every human being. Vedas says " Man will rise above himself surpass himself and reach upto God" This reaching upto God is salvation and is really the purpose and intent of a human being manifesting on Mother Earth.This rising and reaching upto God bestows great powers enjoining upon every human being an inherent duty to sustain protect and preserve nature and all other beings. A human being who has renounced Soul is prone to all evil and goes about doing inhuman activities bringing in chaos and ravaging by going against nature, natural ways, and means. Going against nature is a factor that degenerates and erodes of humanness in humans making them evil and monotonously despotic without sentiments and human values. In circumstances and atmospheres riddled by unnatural activities and attitudes, economic well-being and freedoms cant survive and will succumb to miseries and agony.These dispositions of renunciation of soul abuse and selling body one can see rampantly among narcissists and gays bringing in catastrophic disposition in economic equality and well being strenuously going for one man up prominence with the profit motive as the only criteria for personal even familial relations and connections making humanity like androids devoid of humanness.This sole consideration of profits and molding of humans on the lines of profit-orientedness as ways and aims in life destroys the humanness ravaging the sacred family relationships of parents and children as well as siblings striking the death knell to humanness and the Unity of humanity.

A person solely going about with the purpose and aim of earning profits as is in the cases of trained businesspersons and entrepreneurs if they don't change and bring about a metamorphosis in their priorities making it their duty aim and purpose to strive for the general wellbeing and good of the people, are not suited for managing Government agencies and organizations meant and constituted solely for securing the welfare wellbeing and good of the people without any desire for striking an advantage or profit in the process. When a finance minister of a nation goes about relying on parrot learned and taught stultified principles of economics intended to secure and provide unfair gains by way of incentives to even enterprises without any bonafide as to sustainability and viability with a sole motive of making profits some way or other will bring in doom to the general public good and wellbeing. Especially so when these biased and unreasonable measures are taken and continued ignoring the realities of the situations brought about by the applications of these unfair and unconscionable economic measures supposedly and ostensibly intended for bringing about the good of the people, in reality, brings in a chasm of disparity of income and wealth among the people. Whatever be the theories or however their coining If in practice these theories perpetrate not good results as can be assessed by common sense if becomes a necessity to go for introspection and take measures to correct the maladies. Anyone with common sense and prudence will vouchsafe the introspection and rethinking as a compulsory necessity for the situations so as to make the measures vibrant in achieving the object and purpose for which it is brought about and the measures are taken. The same applies to any theories or measures intended to secure The Good of humanity. It is by these measures of prudence and commonsense of suitable corrections to practices and concepts for bringing about th4e desired effect intended that Humanity has been able to progress from the Era of The Rule of Jungel to present times situations of The Rule of law. It is these trial errors and remedies that enable humanity to correct drawbacks and surge forward till now. Anyone who opposes these corrective measures and introspection is in reality retarding the progress of humanity. The Capitalist economics nowadays propagated by Capitalist economics and capitalist oriented organizations like the International Monetary fund etc will only bring in furtherance of the capitalistic Billionaires not the Large majority of common people further pushing the common people to the position of being the nourishment and accessories for augmenting creation of wealth and as a market for sustaining Billionaires wealth and ways of life living in pathetic conditions and miseries. Applying the God given reasoning power to the realities perceived by the senses and intelligence humanity brought in a combination of capitalistic and welfare economies thereby manifesting the progressive and futuristic viable concept of a mixed economy. This is a remarkable achievement or rather milestone in the progress of humanity towards the ultimate achievable economic system based on Dharma or good of Humanity as Dharmaism espousing and bringing about the concept of " Reasonable and Fair returns "to anyone and everyone. One who spends says a hundre4d should get reasonably worth of hundred commodity or service or returns for the money spending and vice versa for anything the person does thereby avoiding exploitation and cheating by anyone.

Dharmaism in Socioeconomic and political management of Humanity is adopting anything and everything that is good and promotes sustainable Good and wellbeing of humanity in general eschewing everything that is bad. When only two ways results in pursuing a way One a little bit not so good and the other largely bad that has to be accepted which brings the least bad. In choosing a way to be adhered to from two or three or diverse The one that brings in the least or minimal harm has to be chosen.Going by these one comes face to face with the necessity of discarding practices of sheer profitability of public utility services and endeavor about emphasizing the necessity of General public good even if some losses are incurred in the process.. Here the only common yardstick of Dharmsism springs up as the ideal for establishing and achieving the common Good of Humanity.In securing the collective Good of humanity or Dharma even the individual acts activities and deeds of individuals matter and affects the wellbeing and progress in peace and prosperity of the humanity as a whole bringing about a situation that when the Karma of individuals is harmful for the collective or common Good of humanity or general public naturally restrictions to make the action or activities in conformity with the necessity fo general public good comes in as necessities. This is what people's Governments democratically elected and established for the good of people should as a duty strive and persevere to achieve. Otherwise, Government will be placed in the juxtaposition of the object and purpose for what they are brought into being namely The GOOD of PEOPLE. These antipeople activities by Governments and governmental organizations bring in inhumanness and miseries to all. With these factors in mind, one has to assess the disinvestment drive of the Governments in the name of profitability of public utility services and undertakings. Public utility services and other concerns of the Government catering to the needs of providing basic necessities and furthering freedoms even if running on a little loss or some losses have to be sustained in consideration of the important sustenance and impetus they provide in the making available of provisions for the full exercise of peoples basic freedoms and necessities for making human life wholesomely Good.Take for example The Defense industries No one gives much about the profitability of defense industries catering to the defense need of the nations. Why is it so that profitability is not given much importance in the establishment and operation of defense industries .ISNT IT THAT THEY ARE NECESSARY TO THE SUSTANINACE FO THE NATION ITSELF AS A DETERRENT TO OTHERS NOT TO EMBARK UPON AN EVIL ADVENTURE IMPINGING UPON THE EXISTENCE OF THE NATIONS ITSELF.It is the necessity to secure the security and existence of the Nation or county that defense industries are maintained in spite of making huge losses. This is the same in the case of aeronautical and space agencies for Governments. Similarly, necessities are there to sustain public utility services and concerns providing basic services to enable people to live comfortably and happily in freedoms has to be maintained even if runnion of some losses in consideration of the great public supports and inputs they provide making their lives of the general public meaningfully wholesome and okay. The mixed economies of Norway, Sweden, etc are made among the best places where humans can live happily and comfortably in peace and prosperity are Mixed economies bring out the best available in the economic management of the world's nations. Norway comes first on the scale of somewhat happy Nations of the world giving to its people a good standard of living and well-being in prosperity. Here one finds that all do not go about or are managed on a profit-motivated purpose or object. In the case of public utility services the concern and purpose should not be profit-oriented nor the desire to secure a profit in the balance sheet. The main object or aim should be to provide the essential services to the people of the nations with an earnest effort to strike a break-even balance sheet if possible with some reserves the rest will become and will have to be added on in view of the services rendered for the Good and happiness of the people. Achieving this will place these concerns among the best profit-making concerns of the world considering the services these concerns provide to humanity in maintaining their wellbeing and necessities of life. Abandoning public services and handing over these public utility services to the private entrepreneurs and concerns will bring in sheer profit orientation and motivated management into these services determinantal to the good and wellbeing of humanity moved by the only yardstick of profits whatever and however manner possible ending up in the exploitation of the people.This is not n conformity and consonance with the aim and purposes for which democratically elected Governments are brought into existence. On the contrary, these ways of economic management bings about paradoxical situations perverting the very purpose of democracy and the Good of the people making the Goivernemtns fall to the position of company management interested in only bringing about a profit and reserves in the balance sheets of the nations discarding the aim of peoples Good progress in prosperity and well-being. It is in these circumstances that one has to evaluate the Gharmic all pervading concept of Hindutva " Do unto others as you would do unto you " The not so good evil attitude that only profits matter or suffice will degenerates humans to a lowly level of beasts acting on an instance of mere profits detaching oneself of the humanness and divinity inherent within every human being making them inhuman ravaging the collective unity and Good of all humanity. In providing essential necessities Governments and governmental agencies should not be governed by sheer profit motives. This does not mean that Governmental departments and agencies should not be efficient and vibrant smartly and effectively doing and pursuing their work and doing their duty of sincerely striving for the purposes they are employed.The inefficiency and ineffectiveness of Governmental departments and agencies are due to the lethargic indifference and lack of concern and sincerity as a duty in striving for achieving the purposes of people Good coined as purposes of these organizations, in the minds of the people manning these institutions. When Governmental organizations and agencies are motivated by sheer profit motives they ignore the basic duty inherent in them of providing services to the people for their good and wellbeing. Profit motives in everything will only help billionaires and their exploitative attitudes and tactics of whatever happens a profit has to be driven in and obtained bringing in a monotonous mechanical approach deprived of sentiments of humanness moved by a motive of making money whatever happens and however the means pursued ensuring catastrophic inhumanness and evils in the world.

These attitudes bring in even commercialization of familial relationships and human comradeship connections sounding the death knell of unity of humanity impinging upon the collective progress of humanity as a whole unitedly. As The collective well-being and Good of humanity are hampered by the mean and evil actions and activities of a person or group of persons moving on the lines of profiteering and exploitation giving a go by to the ultimate goal of securing the wellbeing and good of humanity it becomes a necessity that such actions ahs to be curbed and nipped int he bud so that humanity as a whole unitedly will flourish in Good. To make Governemtnal organizations vibrant and efficiently competent for achieving the aims for which these organizations are brought into being it is necessary to see that personnel manning these august organizations work in sincerity or preserve to see that people's problems are solved somehow in accordance with legally permissible ways and means rather than continued without solutions. These have to be the guiding factor in providing services to the people and should be imbibed into everyone employed or going about as public servants or officials. Lackluster and inefficient attitudes and dispositions created by employers and employees in public organizations that whatever happens even if they idle away time without working they will get salary at eh end of the month has to go and should be replaced with sincerity and earnestly to see to it that work is done efficiently and sincerely providing solutions for the people's issues effectively and properly fast. It is the atmosphere and attitudes of Government concerns created by its vested interests that whatever happens even if one works or doesn't work one will get a salary that has to be curtailed more so when one realizes the reality that many Government officials go on delaying the settlement of people issues and goes on delaying the settlement or solving of simple issues in the hope that the concerned parties will come to them and grease their palms and they will be immensely profited motivating these and others to go in these lines with the profit motive as the end bringing in ineffectiveness and catastrophic failure of August vibrantly constituted Govenremtnal concerns for bringing about the good progress in peace and prosperity of the people in happiness. The delaying and dilly-dallying tactics of Public officials in the hope and consequential running of people to them and giving them bribes for doing what has to be done forthwith in accordance with law and conventions will only serve to commercialize corruptions and bring miseries to people making and establishing corruption as a away to earn profit and prominence in society. This brings in deceit and fraud for obtaining what is desired thereby criminalizing the society and rampantly ravaging humanity as a whole. Nowadays one finds evil people with a vested interest of helping private concerns conspiring with private entrepreneurs and permeating into public concerns by providing public utility services with the sole intention of sabotaging the working of the concern so as to make it appear that these Public utility services are inefficient at providing efficient services to the people and driving people to go away form these public utility services for availing of the services provided at a higher rate by private concerns thereby bringing in the downfall of these august services. This one finds in Governmental public utility services like bsnl providing internet connectivity. These technicians intending o help private enterprises cut off-net connectivity now and then saying it's server trouble and makes people fed up with these attitudes and forcing them to switch to other private concerns for a higher exploitative price thereby shattering the good public institution's viability and existence. These are practiced in mobile connectivity by ingenious persons sabotaging public utility services to help the private exploitative concerns success and profitability. The necessity and need of the house and times is not to abandon public utility services but to see that the evils that are hampering the viability and success of these august institutions have to be identified and eradicated so that they will thrive in their duty of service to the humanity. On these one finds that it's the quality of people manning these institutions that determine their effectiveness and success. Employment of Honest decent people with an inclination to efficiently do what is enjoined as their duty without fear or favor only will help to eradicate the maladies facing public utility services and make than vibrantly effective for bringing about the purpose for which they are brought into being. Thus it is an imperative necessity to streamline all public utility institutions and bring about a situation making all employees accountable and liable and sincerely work in accordance with the duties and aims of the concern earnestly and sincerely working in the hours of work providing solutions to peoples problems and issues in accordance with law and conventions achieving the object tot the concern for the good of people.This the conclusion inevitable is that the success of a concern depends upon the attitudes attributes and the resolve of duty in the purposes of the persons who man it and power it to move on.Proper supervision by competent honest officers has to be provided so s to make it certain that workers work properly. When delinquent proper inquiry has to be conducted and the delinquent given chance to correct and move on otherwise the delinquent has to be removed from the concern and good personnel brought in so as to serve as a deterrent in the realization of the goals for which the public utility services are brought into being. Strict adherence to service-orientedness for achieving the good of the people and quickly solving people's issues and problems alone will make Governemtns organizations and agencies people friendly and achieve the goals for which they are constituted. As is evident these maladies cant be eradicated except by bringing in-laws to make these delinquencies punishable with punitive compensation to the affected public persons. Public utility services personnel making illegal endeavors and activities has to be made accountable and Ghovernetn has to provide vindictive damages and compensation to the affected instaniously as a deterrent to all so as to force restrain on illegal activities in public utility services and Governmental services. The working motto of Government servants and officials including public utility services should be to somehow provide the service within the framework of law and not to deny service or facility on some pretext of nonexistent imaginary issue.In present days one finds that the tendency of many Government services and agencies is to somehow deny the facilities and services except when proper greasing of palms by way of bribes or recommendations from higher-ups or bigwigs comes.The4se are the main causes of failures of vibrant institutions contrived and made realities for bringing about the good, progress in peace and prosperity of people . This brings one to the realities of Governmental agencies and organizations intended for the securing of financial well-being and prosperity otherwise of humanity is very well-meant and Theoretically vibrant and effective in bringing about the aim and purpose of their being brought into existence.Unfortunately, no one gives much thought to the actual facts bringing about a catastrophic failure and contra effect and inefficacy in the working of these institutions. Why do these well-intended and far-sighted futuristic public institutions fail in achieving the object of their coming into being. The natural reason that comes in as reality is that the personnel who manage and man these institutions are dishonest corrupt and incompetent to man the institutions meant to bring about a metamorphosis of humanity in the quest for progress to yonder levels of prosperity especially so as they or most of them do not do their duty with a sense of service orientedness humanness and sincerity. These are also the outcome of political parties and corrupt official higherups in rank not taking much action to curb, curtail and prevent the indifferent attitudes and make their personnel work properly or kick them out of the concern. Bringing about these levels of disciplinary strictness will make these institutions productive subserving the aim and purpose of public good intended by these institutions.In concluding one is confronted with the stark reality of the obvious truth that the success and purpose of achieving the effectiveness of any concern or organization entirely depend and is wedded upon the quality of the person and personnel who man these concerns and who control these institutions from the helm. Effe4ctiveness can be achieved only by employing people who are honest, and open-minded having thorough knowledge in their respective working spears with an inclination to go by law in all cases and instances.On the contrary when the personnel especially the persons who in the helm of things managing the concern are not having a thorough knowledge of their respective spears of activities will only deceitfully and fraudulently bring in ineffectiveness dishonesty and incompetence thwarting the very purpose for which the organizations are brought into being. Nowadays with the increasing trade and commerce to manifold extends igniting disputes and differences requiring resolutions and decisions Courts or Judiciary comes into prominence as a necessity as a cardinal factor helping in resolving disputes and contentions aiding and augmenting the smooth progress of economic activities for human betterment and progress in prosperity. The Judiciary assumes importance in view of the duty inherent in all democratically functioning countries accepted all pervading principles of proclaimed Economic equality to their people so s to promote humanness and fraternity in peaceful progress and prosperity. Economic equality implies that all humans are basically equal and as equals basically in spite of having different capacities and capabilities, reasonings, aspirations, and aims are entitled to basic necessities so that they can live comfortably giving much time to the pursuit of excellence in their respective spears of actively. Even the directive principles o State Policy as enshrined in Article 39 A of The Constitution of Indai say that no one shall be deprived of accessibility to courts of law meaning for determination of assertions of rights infracted because of his financial or other disabilities. Article 39 (b) says that the ownership and material resources of the community are so distributed so as to subserve the common good. 39 (C) that the operation of the economic system does not result in the concentration of wealth and means of production to the common detriment. Thus Judiciary has a cardinal duty to see that economic equality is there for equally placed groups of people or groups of people as the case may be. This economic equality basically implies that all humans have to be treated as a group basically being humans and given or provided basic essentials for a proper livelihood enabling all to live reasonably and fairly in pursuance of higher levels of progress in prosperity and prominence in excellence thereby catapulting humanity to the highest levels of progress achievable. The Judiciary being a catalyst brought into being for achieving the goals of economic equality has to play a pivotal role in bringing into being economic equality by helping resolve disputes in accor4aqnce with the legal principles and rules of law applicable honestly and reasonably fairly. Rule of law gives a yardstick for everyone to arrange their affairs of conduct for business and enter into contracts and partnerships in furtherance of commercial and financial activities. Law is said to be certain uniform consistent and definite and anyone who goes by law has to get a decision in success as per the law Naturally courts while actually rendering decisions, especially in commercial matters are augmenting the economic progress of the country. Any dishonest Judicial officers going against the law and legal principles and deciding the list in a lackluster manner on fanciful surmises and conjectures giving a ago by to law and legal principles deceitfully and dishonestly are bringing about uncertainties in economic activities thereby retarding the progress of humanity shattering the concept of equality in all respects and aspects of life.In accordance with the time tested principles of rule of law it assumes significance as a duty cast on everybody as well as oneself to see that Only persons who are honest, open-minded, thorough in law with an inclination to go by law in all cases alone should be appointed and should man the positions of Judicial officers whatever. Nowadays with no certain enumerated and defined criteria for determining the qualifications of a judicial officer an enumeration of the basic necessities for being considered for appointment as a Judicial officer is extremely necessary and an unavoidable need of the times so as to subserve the cause of equality and Justice in all spears of humanity's life.Only these measures will bring in a metamorphosis making The Judiciary effective and vibrant for ensuring Justice to all making reality the very purpose of establishing and sustaining the Justice system for Good of humanity. Apart from these anyone going contra to these basic necessities has to be given a warning to correct their ways to suit the Judicial office then maybe another reprimand or censure if not amenable dismissal and retribution have to ensue. Th4ese seems to be the only way out for any institution or organization to rise to the levels contemplated for fulfilling the duties and purposes for which they are brought into being. The attributes and qualities of the personals manning the institutions and organizations concerned being important and cardinal in bringing about the desired results and cardinal in bringing about the desired results purposes and aims for bringing about these august organizations' realities. When going by disciplinary ways to bring in necessary results The Top persons manning these institutions when found delinquent has to be dealt with strictly in a manner that these delinquencies won't be repeated.

In these matters, one or everyone can draw enlightenment from the Divinelogic of Bhagavat Geetha wherein Sri Krishan in the course of disclosures by way of divine logic to Arjuna says " What Shrestha Purush does others imitate ". That is what persons of eminence and prominence respect as Shreshta does others who are common people have a tendency to imitate and personify. Here Shreshta in ordinary parlance means respected or revered persons. Actually, Shrestha's position has to be earned and achieved by one's pious deeds and activities. But unfortunately for a child, one finds that whatever his father is maybe a thief but for him, his father is an important Shrestha purush and the child tends to imitate and emulate whatever his father does. This inclination or tendency for a child to keenly observe and imitate his father in ways and means are there in everyone who considers some other persona his idol or shreshta purush. Thus a child will easily show how his father smokes or go about doing things etc so goes the general people's psychology bringing in the necessity of punishing as an example anyone who is Shrestha if they commit crimes and fraudulent activities of deceit and delinquencies. These disciplinary attitudes have to be adopted in streamlining the public concerns and organizations so as to make them people-oriented and bring about the purpose and object of their being brought into existence. Any attitudes which bring in miseries and ravage of the wellbeing and good fo humanity ahs to be dealt with as hereinbefore provided so that these maladies will be curbed in the but without any attraction for repetition thereby achieving the smooth running of concerns for the good of people.

Now we find that Nations are managed as if they are companies Vis kids from multinationals come in control or are brought into control of every aspect of Governmental functioning on the pretext of increasing efficiency and running the country on a profitable basis. Now is the country to be managed on profit motive as a private company that too by the supposed people's representatives inherently for achieving the good of people. Profit motive management serves in achieving a profit in the balance sheet by whatever methods are employed. In these aspects, the accounts assume significance and are important but are these the criteria for managing a country. In these ways, only profit is given the prominence even public utilities and service orientedness vanish giving way to striking a balance in accounts giving up even humanness and welfare orientation for governments services intended for the good of people. With the advent of profit-oriented management in Government giving up people's welfare, we find public utility services whereby Government provide essential services to people as imposed by their duty, sold to private enterprises so as to make it profit-oriented and exploitative for the people instead of being a machinery for serving the pole for securing their wellbeing and welfare. Public utility services even if they make some losses are worth their value in Gold as they provide essential services to the people so that they can exercise their freedoms effectively and be happy. Securing a breakeven is a good or excellent performance for these concerns in view of their providing basic essential services which the peoples Governments have to provide as a duty. These profit orientedness has radically changed human nature also as all are after profits and quick money what more when one finds even The Government of the people by the people interested only in profit achieving and not good of people as is contrary to the proclaimed principles of democratic governments exposition in being peoples Governments by the people's representatives. To find true human love one has to search much as earning wealth and money is the only criteria nowadays recognized as one's prominence and progress in society. Everyone tries to grab some money by hook or crook bringing into existence and rampant prominence dilly-dallying and hankey Pankey behavior bringing up deceitful and fraudulent practices for achieving the mean object of wealth amassment so as to attain prominence and respect in society. One can find these even among laborers. They work slowly and with dilatory tactics to work for ten days where the work can actually be finished in five days thereby fraudulently earning double the money. In even Goivernemtn offices one finds these profit orientations for securing a profit whatever ways are employed. In these lines of working Government offices, one finds that the officla drives people from pillar to post finding out some imaginary errors in their applications or dispositions saying that it's all necessary driving them crazy for not getting their things done in accordance with law and conventions making the people come to them again and again for the same things with corrections and alterations. But if the hands of these officials are greased with some stipulated money everything especially the errors vanishes and the things materialize easily and are given instantly. The prices of petroleum go up and the companies pressurize the Government to rise the prices bringing in an all-round rise in prices causing inflation. But when the prices recede the raised prices are not brought back thereby causing deceitful loss to people. What is lacking is humanness. Dharma has vanished and everything is measured in terms of the money one has or makes. These tendencies have eroded the virtues of being human and driven people to lowly evil habits. Deceit and fraudulent ways are becoming ways of life and are tolerated widely by even police personnel and Judicial officers. These finds support when one persues the huge hoardings that were there on the eastern side overhead foot overbridge in which it's written: " When deceit and lies have become ways of life Its Revolution to speak the truth ". These vehemently show the extent of degeneration of truth in society. To change this degeneration the first thing that has to be done is to change the way of profit orientation in the management of Nations nations and see to it that Nations are managed in a holistic and welfare way so that people come first even if the balance sheet shows some deficit or losses or just even an excellent breakeven. These levels of Governmental functioning will permeate to all and pervade to instill confidence in people to change their attitudes towards life and their fellow human beings bringing in an optimistic positive disposition in all matters stealing humanness and unity of humanity. The feeling that after all, we are all basically human beings will come into predominance and get strengthened achieving a common bonding yardstick for unity.In theory, everything is good and safe but when it comes into practice all goes wrong, and in the name of practicality every theory propounded for humanity's good is given a go by bringing in contra results. Here one finds that what is the need for the house and times is the adhering to Theories in all aspects in practice so that the intended results come in for benefit of all. " Theoretical perfection practically achieved is the best that can be achieved ", and is the only acceptable principle that can be made use of in all spears. The only exceptions are when the theory itself is wrong and stultified by vested interests to bring about paradoxical dispositions necessitating a compulsorily rethinking and introspection so as to correct the mistakes and make it a vibrant instrument of social progress and the Good of humanity.

Nowadays even finance ministers of great Countries are doctorate degree holders and go by these faulty theories propounded to secure and sustain the wealth of the rich and super-rich leading to further concentration of wealth and money in the hands of few going to the extent of even stultifying the proclaimed Constitutions mandates sought to be realized by molding even laws conducive to these principles of Consitution. Applying these parrot learned defective theories proved to be wrong by experiences and common sense in the management of finance of countries ignoring the paradoxical manifestations experienced successively for decades brings in only miseries to ordinary people by rising in prices of essential commodities and life's expenses without a commensurate rise in income. People. who are supposed to be pseudo economic specialists goes on repeating the applications of these theories shattering even the constitution's mandates of fair distribution of wealth and resources thereby bringing in only economic inequality as well as an increasing chasmic gap of disparity of wealth and income. Think of it The Malthusian concept that while population increases in Geometrical progression Food production increase only in arithmetical progression bringing in the reality that there is a possibility of population outshooting food production thereby bringing in chances of food scarcity has been proved to be not that effective by adopting the advanced scientific methods of agriculture, farming, and techniques. This proposition has been made inapplicable by the united effort of humanity in adopting and applying scientific approaches in the spear of agriculture and food production in the world as a whole. This has made i9t possible to increase food production to a level of more than sufficient to feed the ever-rising population. Now we can be satisfied with the reality of food production is more than sufficient to feed the world population. This is a reality of tremendous progress achieved by humanity unitedly showing that the principles of economics can go wrong to an extent by adopting scientific advancement and approaches in agriculture and farming. These testify to the reality that humanity can achieve many things supposed to be impossible when unitedly surging forward as these are humanity's progress of par excellence to the extent of even making part of an economic law ineffective at times wherein scientific advancement of realities are made use of and the ill effects of even theories warded off. Here one finds that The Theory propounded by Malthus coined a Malthusian theory of populations has been rendered ineffective by the experiences of humanity standing unitedly and adopting advanced scientific methods of agriculture and farming. But in the normal ordinary progress of humanity deprived of scientific advancements and inventions applying the inquisitive temper of humanity in pursuing doubts and suspicions these principles of Malthus will be true and correct applying always. The latter part of Malthusian there of population says that When the population increases enormously without proper checks and controls Nature brings in natural checks and controls in the way of natural calamities so as to bring about the negation of the unwanted populations.

These are natural calamities brought about by nature not by human misadventures. The opponents of Malthus put forth the contention that even in advanced countries where there is no population explosion or problems there are natural disasters that bring about the death of people. If one reason as a matter of common sense one finds that humanity taken unitedly as a whole has increased tremendously and whatever decreases will be made good by migration from other areas thereby bringing the one part of the Malthusian population correct. It is in this context of making ineffective theories of economics by humans standing unitedly applying progress to achieve excellence in living conditions making certain economic concepts ineffective under certain conditions that one has to view the instruments made use fo for bringing in fair distribution of wealth and control money markets. By experiences, one finds that these instruments have been contrived to only bring in unfair distribution and accumulation of wealth at the cost of miseries and exploitation of the general public it is just prudence and common sense that these practices have to be discontinued and effective defect free practices brought into being by curing the mistakes and shortcomings so as to make these economic measures more people friendly and effective for bringing about a fair and reasonable distribution of income and wealth among the people. These aspects bring in for introspection the policies and measures inducted and made applicable in order to see that the tall proclamations and broad propositions for bringing about an end to the disparity of income and giving an impetus to development are really effective for the purposes they are employed. Take for instance the massive impetus provided by way of concessions and rebates for establishing and running industries and companies. Until recently there were no committees or organizations for seeing to it whether the proposed industries or companies are really necessary and viable . But now in India Honoraberl Prime Minsiter Narendra Modejee has constituted a body to oversee as to whether the proposed investment proposals for establishing industries etc are really genuine and viable. Earlier the situation was any number of the same concerns could get the concessions and incentives for establishing companies and establishments. It was like say ten hotels coming up when money three will be viable and necessary. So ten hotels come up al then is superb and has been brought into being by government incentives and concessions all come up and becomes reality ..people will say want a development there are now ten hotels will superb and this is the sort of development that has to come....but after some time due to the viability factor and the cut-throat completion all fails within say five years of coming into being more so as they are cannot sustain the ten hotels for there is not people requiring the services fo ten hotels so all ten fails and maybe two or three marginally exists and when the others wind up business the remaining may survive but the development is all wasted and what about the Government incentives and concessions all ends up in waste. Whose money is these that is wasted isn't it the people's money and ultimately it's the people who lose. The same happens in the case of industries in the name of development Government offers huge concessions and people with an inclination to make quick money gather in with projects etc of course all need concessions in interest and other incentives all st up the same or similarly same concerns and finally with the un viability factor coming up almost all end up in loses and wither off by the time they wind up the entrepreneurs would have earned more than what they initially invested earing a huge profit vide Government incentives and concessions. So finally it's the people who lose and their income and standard of living suffer. This is senseless misguided development efforts nowadays rampantly seen thwarting the progress of humanity. What is really necessary and should be brought about is sustainable progress or development. The question that comes up for consideration and assessment is whether the management of money markets by Governments and other economic agencies are really bringing about the fair distribution of income and wealth or are they really going contradictory to the avowed tall proclamations of the Peoples Governments, especially as is heralded by The Constitutions of the democracies of the World namely fair distribution of incomes and wealth and standards of living conducive to the good of people and humanity in general. Take the instance of the Government of India nowadays strenuously endeavoring to augment development by encouraging setting up all production concerns in India itself giving huge incentives and concessions. Of course, with the establishment of the watchdog committee in eliminating unwanted fraudulent enterprises only bringing in shattering the well-run business and manufacturing concerns having been brought By The Honorable Primeminister Narendra Modejee working people much erosion of people's wealth and money to fraudulent trojan horses type concerns will stand eliminated bringing in sustainable development and progress.This si the situation that will be there if the committee is working properly and vibrantly ....Otherwise the disturbing situation of the nation's wealth or people's wealth and money being squandered and robbed still persists. Take for instance The motor car manufacturing concerns. Here one has found Government encouraging say ten car manufacturing concerns all viving with one another to sell their cars as best in spite fo all having almost the same efficiency and qualities. Cars are luxuries for the majority of people and think of it nowadays it's really saddening to find car travel in cities and metros really not only tiresome and time-consuming but also bringing in to an extent squandering of wealth for showing off opulence in snobbery and dandiness. The majority of peoples needs only public transport but uses cars of this type and that type bringing enormous pollution and fuel bills for Governments thereby wasting natural resources and adding to the global warming. Now under the pretext of development Governments gives huge incentives for car manufacturing concerns with lucrative offers of cheap loans at concessions rates for interests, land concessions in power,raw materials all totaling to a huge sum ...Concessiond in workers' welfare measures are also granted so as to bring in as many as car manufacturing concerns as possible.This is for the encouragement of development and lo all car manufacturing concerns come in rising especially some of their people who want o earn a quick buck cashing in on concessions and lucrative offers irrespective fo the fact that so many car manufacturing concerns are not really necessary and the coun try will not be able to sustain so much of these concerns especially in according to the people's needs requirements. Ten or more car manufacturing or assembly units are brought into the country ..wow what a great development the Government has brought about, especially by using the scarce resources of the nation intended to secure the welfare of the people for seeing to it that the people live comfortably. By the time cars starts to come out Government would have expended millions or billions as concessions and lucrative grants. This is a real problem when one finds that the concessions given in this way and that way would be much more than the money brought in by the companies and what happens with say a five year period the entrepreneurs would have appropriated much more than what they brought in as capital from Govenremental grants and concessions leaving them with their profit motives satiated. So no problem even if the concerns start making losses and finally coming to a standstill as unviable as by the coming into a varied models fo cares all catering to luxurious modes of transportation and the congestion fo rads with the attendant impossibility of driving easily on roads also with the attending high cost of travel by cars and insurances people are not buying cars with the saturation of market conditions as no one wants cars people do not need so many cars as so many cars are not needed for the people in the market bringing in the sustainability of so many cars not necessary in the market is at stake. In the resulting situation, many car companies collapse bringing in the loss of all the public money given by the government as huge incentives and concessions. This is what will ensue when without any thought to the necessity and sustainability of concerns they are brought in indiscriminately without any thought of necessity and for sustainability .So all these car concerns start to feel the pinch and they approach the government for help saying that cars are not being bought by people and there is the possibility of car companies collapsing. What does the Govenermetn do They bring about the policy change that all cars over say ten years or say fifteen years old should be scraped ....ha ha ha ha All cars above fifteen years in age are taken for scraping and cant be used on the roads... So what do the people do they have to find the money for buying new cars if they really need cars. The government will say that are giving loans for people to buy cars and so let them buy cars ... Ultimat4ely who is losing and being exploited Isn't it the people whose money is wasted that too by abusing the powers of the government. More so when one finds that the process of recycling the used cars will produce and bring in more harmful substances that when they are repaired and used as far they will run efficiently. These are all development bringing activities of supposed Governments who are coming into being for the people's good and who are elected by the people. This will be the case in other essential spears of economic activities when too many people or entrepreneurs set up the same or rather same concerns bringing the question of viability and unsustainability. In these situations, more than economic principles prudence and commonsense will enable people to see to tit that public money is not wasted on unwanted things. In these situations employing the statistical concepts with economic requirements, the exact viability of anything can be correctly assessed and ascertained so as to help the conclusions of sustainability and permissions. Development or progress should always be sustainable progress or development momentary progress for some time and then recanting to prior levels are not worth adhering to nor advisable for good of people and the nations. Otherwise, it will result in waste and loss of all scarce resources of The world intended for the good of the people. In these measures, Honorable Primeminister Sree Narendra Modejee's efforts are laudable in bringing about an expert Goalkeepers committee. But the purpose will be thwarted if these bodies aren't that of expert people incorruptible using economic ways of statical evaluations in determining the sustainability of concerns. In these cases, the use of prudence and commonsense are the only necessities for sure success preventing the wastage of money meant for peoples good.

Are the instruments process and measures adhered to and used by the Government and finance departments to increase the availability of cheap finance for financing Growth and development really meant to safeguard the rich from amassing more money and wealth bringing about the malady of concentration of wealth in the hands of a few to the detriment of the large general public. Is The malady of concentration of wealth in the hands of a few as is seen rampantly in capitalistic countries as well as everywhere the result of defective Government-assisted policies and law for controlling and managing finance and wealth of nations. In the name of providing cheap and concessional finance at very low-interest rates to multinationals and business concerns for commercial purposes on the concept of slashing interest rates on small savings and deposits in public institutions, especially banks accepted and brought about from the public really a good way or is it condemnable as oppressive and exploitative of the general people bringing in miseries and difficulties for the general public. Small savings schemes and Fixed deposits generally belong to the financially not well off people who are not so rich coming within the category of common people who in the middle ages or evening of life are faced with the problems of no work and income or not able to work and no income to meet the daily necessities of life. These problems are tried to be overcome by common people by savings and deposits accumulated while they were working hard so as to be able to get some income by way of interests monthly or quarterly or even yearly enabling these classes to have some income to meet the necessities of life without depending on others when they have no work or are unable to work. When interests on these savings and deposits are slashed without any warning or permission from these depositors it is their capacity to meet the necessities of life that si thwarted and these unfortunate people are put to real miseries and difficulties. when one comes to know that these harsh measures are undertaken at the time of inflation that is rising prices one can easily understand that their purchasing power is curtailed making them unable to buy even sufficient necessities for a comfortable day-to-day living. These measures actually destablishing and common people from even meeting their necessities in life for enabling providing cheap concession to the super-rich is rather sadistically cruel and tend to belittle the common man so as to favor the rich in helping make more wealth at the expense and exploitation of the general public and common people These diabolically cruel measures on the pretext of development financing that too from democratically elected Governments who are said to be peoples representatives duty-bound to bring about policies for the good of people and supposedly bringing about measures for the good of people for the people by the people becomes rather diabolically inhuman when the cumulative effects brings in miseries and difficulties to the general public.This is daylight stealing of money hard-earned with the aid of illegal ways and laws contrived by the deceptively cunning in the organizations so as to bring about the good of only a few vested interests thereby causing the disappearance of purchasing capacity of the general public depriving them of even catering to the securing of necessities of life as are corollaries fo reduced capacity for buying and living comfortably. Money will be there only to support the affluent living of the rich and super-rich as they won't be much affected by this inflation and rescissions brought about by the economic misadventures of the finance departments and institutions of the supposed peoples Govenremtn working in the not desired manner.Just in the name of providing cheap finance to the entrepreneurs and business concerns who earn profits to the tune of hundreds of fo percents in one go thereby making manifold hundreds or thousands of fo percents of profits say in one year is rather disturbing and harmful for the common people.When cheap finance is available on the asking in the name of development impetus fraudsters come in or rush in to make a quick buck taking advantage of the defective policies. They bring in millions and take out billions this si when one looks into the fact that some millions brought in will get incentives and finance with concessional interest rated fo say four percent per annum when actually market rates are say twelve percent. This there is a margin of eight percent. When calculated for a four-year period these concessional rates alone will make the investment double coupled with other incentives within a period of say ten years the concerns will get much more than what they brought in as initial investments. Thus these fraudsters who set up unviable concerns bring in millions and take out billions thereby further reengaging the already hard-pressed common man whose money these people are fleeching with government help and support.

Growth cannot go on indefinitely in one product or products, especially by the operation of the law of Economics of The diminishing marginal utility or returns Any product when produced in more quantity that is actually required or necessary in the market will bring in losses and when more business concerns are there producing the same product naturally many will fail and become unviable. Resulting in companies set up with assistance from people's money collapsing. The utility that is achieved from growth will become zero if growth is not controlled and goes on and one in one product or commodities by the operation of The law of diminishing marginal utility theory The theory can be explained by considering the reality that when one eats an orange first the satisfaction or utility that one gets from the eating fo the first orange will be greatest and the eating of the second brings a reduced utility so goes on when a situation comes that by eating another orange no utility comes. That is zero utility this is applicable in all cases of human consumption except in the cases of exceptions in these concepts of marginal utility theory that is in the cases of money and power. When growth goes on there comes a point in which there will be no utility from growth resulting in a tapering off and maybe going back into recession or slump except when new variants of the products having or give more benefits or new products or variants of more useful and easy convenient uses to people are found out. Take the instance of cars using petrol flooded in market leading to a glut and many companies crashing as unviable even Ford motors has wound up their activities in India. This will be the case explicitly making it a reality that cars are no more in need as the utility that people get from cars will be zero except when electric and other variants come in giving an impetus to the market conditions This also supports the setting of vigilant organizations competent to determine the necessity or viability of any concern beyond certain limits or numbers. As regards the concessional interest one has to bear in mind that actually, companies earn at least twenty percent of the profit on a single item of a product say by selling a product a company gets twenty percent profit one product is sold on day twenty percent is got many products will be sold daily bringing in twenty percent of profits for each product sold daily. In one month or yearly millions of products will be sold each bringing in twenty percent thus bringing in thousand of percent of profits earning manifold percent of profits. It is from these profits concessional interests ahs to be paid No meaning in reduced interests or concessional rates after the concern goes breakeven and becomes profitable. Making these concerns Providing a twelve percent or a little lesser interest for financing the common people's necessities will not cause any injustice for anyone. Whatever one has to bear in mind is that financing and concessions are provided from money exacted by Government through laws mainly from the vast general public. Cunning organizations catering to the needs of entrepreneurs and billionaires by contriving stealthy instruments and ways to see to tit that only the billionaires interests are protected influencing the Government of the world and making them adhere to cheating mechanisms are rather tragically pathetic especially when one finds that these measures cause the misdirection of the purpose for which the governments are brought into being in democratic nations. The Government which is duty-bound to protect the rights and freedoms of people is made to deprive the people of their hard-earned money and wealth by cunning for the benefit of a few vested interests. No wonder the rich are getting richer, especially the billionaires resulting in the concentration of wealth and incomes in the hands of a few depriving the common man of a decent comfortable living.

Nowadays in present times, one finds the Government as well as supposed economists and financial experts lamenting about rising inflation ensuing rising prices for all commodities and services. The Government had hiked up prices of petroleum products and other products basically essential as well as that of some public service utilities including cooking gas resulting in all-around price rises. Now in 2022 fifth month post-Covid, 19 inflation was say about nearly between seven to eight or so percent The private sector heeding the government's price increases the private sector increased prices to say about double that of the Government bringing in another round of inflation. Now the private transport services threatened the Government that they will stop the services if fair rises are not allowed and The Government allowed fair rises the outcome wow a very good inflation ensured. With the inflation financial ministry and Reserve Bank started that inflation is rising and we have to take measures to control inflation by decreasing the purchasing power of people for that they press for an increase in lending rates of interest and decreasing the interest on small savings and fixed deposits as well s increasing the bank rates so as to bring in short or limited money circulation. These measures bring in a shortage of money for the common people for meeting the price increases of even the essential necessities for meeting their day-to-day expenses in life. These measures initiated to control the interest rates further propel inflation to the highest level say fourteen or say percent. The common people are the hard-hit as they will be the class who are hard hit and find it difficult to make both ends meet. With the increase in interest rates on their loans more difficulties in getting money to pay the bills. With all these measures first increasing the inflation and then in the name of controlling it bringing down the money in the hands of people these pseudo economists created miseries and difficulties for common people as the rich have more than sufficient money to cater to the needs of inflation. Then after all these price increases, there are no price increases so it's tapering off or stagnation so there si into inflation ha ah ha ha seems it's because of these measures that inflation has been controlled and made stationary. Ho, it's because there is no scope for any further price rise the prices stand or remain constant. As people have no money to buy even their essentials necessities the other commodities demand falls and all comes to a sluggish standstill manner so this recession ....Then again to meet the recessionary trends some sops are given to common people and they slowly rise up to the situations and makes up some way out to bring in more money in their hands and so the demands rise and so on and so forth. The business class gets more money from increases or inflation but the thought of where this money is coming from is rather disturbing when one knows that it's the common people who buy these products for the business class and give them more money. Thus business classes are not much affected by this inflation. Whatever it's the vast general public suffers and finds it difficult for meeting their necessities pushing them to perils and miseries. Even their hard-earned savings gets lower interests disabling them to rise to the situation and make both ends meet somehow. Just by rising the petroleum prices, there will be an all-around increase in prices of even the essential commodities enabling common men to meet their expenses in life due to the increase in freight charges and logistics. Prices of petroleum have to be at the highest so as to control unnecessary travel and the squandering of scarce natural resources and as luxurious travel and living are all fuelled by petroleum consumption it's also the best source of development financing. while increasing the petroleum prices if the government gives selective concessions or decreases in fuel prices for the public cargo goods transport sector and logistics will go a great way in keeping the price rise in check.

The general publics' hard-fought and won a majority of savings are all held up in small savings and welfare schemes of Government, especially so as private concerns offering lucrative interest rates have by experiences shown a tendency of vanishing after some years making people lose their money when putting in private concerns lucrative schemes of investment as they have by experiences shown a tendency of vanishing after some time of performing well causing the public to lose their hard-earned money. The government being a democratic government supposedly meant for the people by the people for their good brings in a reasonable and legitimate expectation that the Government schemes are really meant for the welfare of the people and will ensure reasonable and fair returns without any risk of being lost after some time making it more lucrative and safe for common people. It is with these legitimate expectations that common people lock their money in Government schemes with the sole further purpose and intention of securing an income for being a help and support in meeting the daily necessities of life. When the interest of these hard-earned savings is decreased for bringing about a nonsense-like effect it's in effect actually shattering the legitimate expectation of the people by their own governments going against duty. More so when one finds that it's from these small savings and deposits of people's interests cuts and snatching of interest that big and rich billionaires concerns are given concessional rates of interest say four percent enabling them to mint money and add on billions to their already huge coffers. This is fleeching the common public so as to fiance the riches of the billionaires. In these aspects also its " Kudos " to our beloved Primeminsiter of Inda Bahumanya Sree Narendra Modejee who has stood firm on all these measures and refused to decrease the interest rates on small deposits thereby giving a little relief to the common man. Along with these if discounts and concessions are given to cargo and public transport system in fuel prices it will reduce the burden of the common man very much by bringing about the prices of essential commodities and arresting inflation in addition to bringing in needed finance for development from luxurious living people. It is on these realities that one ponders over the realities as to whether the imbalances in incomes and wealth are the result of defective financial policies of governments and whether these need an introspection and correction so as to achieve the good of the general public.

When one views these realities of economics and how it is affecting the everyday lives of people in the context of present times or days realities it becomes a necessity in the interest of public good to bring about a rethinking on an introspection of the principles of economics coupled with the instruments fo money market management so as to ascertain whether these instruments and measures which are used and employed with the professed purpose of achieving a fair distribution of wealth among people for ensuring a reasonably fair standard of living is actually achieving the purpose for which they are employed. This is an apt stage for applying the all-pervading concepts Of Dharma as a yardstick in ascertaining the effect of these principles with respect to igniting the good of people or humanity in general. Dharma applied in economics brings about Dharmaism or the Good of people as the essential primary yardstick or purpose of these principles. Dharmaism seeks the employing of any or all principles that bring in the good of people and the establishment of a reasonably fair Good standard of living for all humanity underlining the need to provide all necessities in life as well as some comforts so as to achieve comfortable living and helping everyone in the pursuit of excellence in life in accordance with one's capacities and capabilities. The teacher here is common sense and prudence combined with everyday experiences in ways of life's progress for ascertaining whether these principles of economics are actually achieving the object for which they are used and adhered to. Finally one has to admit that for Economics and economic principles to enable the bringing about of a reasonable fair and good living conditions the primary necessity that crops up for immediate consideration and action are the maintenance of normal living conditions on Mother Earth. With Global warming and consequent climate change ushering in extreme climatic changes and catastrophic situations, the primary casualty will be the economic activities. The primary purposes of all science and humanities have to be for seeing primarily the Maintainance of normal living conditions and it's only after that the other considerations crop up for adherence and applications for results and aimed ends. A duty inherent is there on everyone to see to it aht living conditions on Mother Earth do not deteriorate to levels causing the ravage of humanity bringing in an obligation on all concerns and industries to innovate and adopt ways and means not harmful to the Mother Earth and normal living conditions on Mother earth. The indiscriminate cutting of trees for mainly avowed commercial purposes has to be stopped and all efforts should be conserved and unified to plant trees so as to be sufficient to bring back all lost forests thereby ensuing in giving back Mother Earth her cooling cap. The significance of a cooling cap can be best understood if one goes and stands in the Sun for five minutes and thereafter go and stand under a shady tree Wah what a coolness it is that's there under the shady trees invigorating life and bringing back the lost zest in oneself. This is what Trees will give to mother earth a cooling cap invigorating life itself and a healthy atmosphere for an excellent living for humanity. Obviously, it's the loss of the cooling cap of Mother Earth that is bringing about the Majority of The global warming and consequent rise in seas because of melting ice on the north pole, etc. Only by bringing back the lost trees that play a vital role in purifying the atmosphere and aiding in the cooling of Mother earth that enables all life to subsist and flourish. There is no possibility of mimicking the work of trees in removing carbon dioxide from the atmosphere and bringing back normal conditions. No other way for humanity to secure economic well-being and welfare by ensuring reasonably fair and good living conditions other than striving and preserving to bring back lost trees and give back Mother Earth her Cooling cap. Anyone who wantonly cuts or destroys trees unreasonably has to be punished as an example so as it will be a deterrent to others A warning not to cut valuable trees. Anyone cutting a tree has to be made to plant at least then trees or maybe lesser in accordance with one's conscience levels . Only these will bring in awareness of the exigencies of the perilous and catastrophic situations prevalent brought about by ingeniously ruffian-minded people unscrupulously destroying the equilibrium maintained by nature for safeguarding precious human life and conditions for humanity to excel and surpass itself reaching up to God in the extreme levels of progress achievable. Comrades " Plant more trees and save humanity from certain perils and catastrophies ".

The only enlightenment that is brought about on an evaluation of the realities of the wealth sharing and distribution ways in the lives of humanity is whatever be the state of unity or wellbeing of the humanity in general. It is the quality of a human being that assumes importance and plays a predominantly determinative role in bringing about the Good, wellbeing, and welfare of the people or humanity in general. As is clear that it is the hypocritic insincere and evil activities of human beings unconcerned by the repercussions that will be brought about, especially in the realization of the whim to acquire wealth and money by ingeniously evil and not good ways that bring in misfortunes endangering humanity pushing the entire welfare and wellbeing of people into perils and miseries One realizes the necessity of adhering to strictly the laws and processes for preventing these misuses giving extreme stress to the prevention and curtailment of thee illegal and not good activities. Whatever be the scientific principles or economic concepts that are formulated and designed for bringing about the Good of humanity as is the laws to prevent the destruction of Trees and forests or prevent pollution everything depends on the honesty and quality of the persons manning the concerns or offices intended to prevent these maladies. The making of adherence to the Rule of law making any activities detrimental to the good of humanity offenses also depend upon the persons or public officials who are man these agencies designated to proceed and apprehend or as the case may be to prevent these illegal activities. It's not the defects of the systems of machinery that impinge upon the good measures and bring about paradoxical effects but the incompetence, dishonesty, and immorality of the people who are responsible to see that these ways are adhered to . Only by appointing honest and open-minded people with a thorough knowledge of areas of operations with an inclination to go by legal principles alone will bring in the desired results

Gadhadharan Punathil
Punathil house
Manipuram lane
Nadakav, Calicut-673011
Kerala State, India